Out
of the
Miry Clay

Susan A. Millican

WestBow
PRESS
A DIVISION OF THOMAS NELSON

WestBow Press books may be ordered through booksellers or by contacting:

WestBow Press
A Division of Thomas Nelson
1663 Liberty Drive
Bloomington, IN 47403
www.westbowpress.com
1-(866) 928-1240

Because of the dynamic nature of the Internet, any web addresses or links contained in this book may have changed since publication and may no longer be valid. The views expressed in this work are solely those of the author and do not necessarily reflect the views of the publisher, and the publisher hereby disclaims any responsibility for them.

Any people depicted in stock imagery provided by Thinkstock are models, and such images are being used for illustrative purposes only.

Certain stock imagery © Thinkstock.

ISBN: 978-1-4497-2605-8 (sc)
ISBN: 978-1-4497-2606-5 (hc)
ISBN: 978-1-4497-2607-2 (e)

Library of Congress Control Number: 2011915525

Printed in the United States of America

WestBow Press rev. date: 9/14/2011

I dedicate this book to:

—My Lord and Savior, Jesus Christ, for dying for me on the cross to cover all of my sins, carrying me through the dark hours, comforting me through the sadness, filling me with His joy and peace, adopting me into His kingdom, and using me to share His great love through the lessons in this book.

—My beloved husband, Billy Lee the love of my life, for showing me how Christ sees me, showering me with Christ unconditional love, and treating me as Christ treats the church!

—My parents, Don and Ann Thornhill, whom I am forever grateful for being a living example that loving Jesus is the most important relationship I can nurture, that sharing His love is the best gift I can give, and extending His grace, and mercy is the best example I can live.

—My sister, Pam McDaniel, for being the best friend ever, loving me through all stages of my life, holding me accountable to Christ, and sharing her beautiful children, Carson and Kameron, with me.

—My brother, David Thornhill, for showing me the difference Christ makes, sharing the Word of God in a manner I can understand, praying me through all the tough times, and being a living example of unconditional love.

—Carla Miller for ALL of her prayers and encouragement for me to stand firm, keep my faith, and wait on Jesus!

—All of my friends who encouraged me to write this book.

I love you and thank you all for being Christ to me! Susan

²He drew me out of the horrible pit (a pit of tumult and of destruction), out of the miry clay (froth and slime), and set my feet upon a rock, steadying my steps and establishing my goings.

Psalm 40: 2 (AMP)

Forward

Nevertheless I am continually with thee: thou hast holden me by my right hand. Psalm 73:23

I met Susan when we began working together in the fall of 2010. She reached out to me on my first day and made me feel welcome and wanted. Her faith was evident even then, but as our friendship deepened, I was impressed with her ability to see God in ordinary, everyday things. I had fallen into a pattern of only seeing God during the "big" events of my life, but Susan always inspires me to look for His presence in my daily life.

These stories reflect Susan's ability to see God in both the "big" and the "little" life events. I hope they inspire you to seek God in both the extraordinary and ordinary events of your life. What a comfort to know that He is continually with us.

God bless,

Jennifer M. Reese

Contents

Introduction

While I was raised in a Christian home and accepted Jesus as my Savior at an early age, it was not until I was pulled out of the horrible pit of sin as an adult that I realized I needed to make Christ more than my Savior. You see, I had invited Jesus into my heart but I put Him in the guest room and only allowed Him to participate in the parts of my life that I chose; you know, the parts that looked and felt good. It wasn't until I was facing my second divorce that I realize I needed more than just a Savior if I was ever going to get my house in order. At this point I knew I had to surrender to Jesus the rest of my house and make Him Lord and Ruler over my life.

It was during this time that I decided if I was going to surrender, I better get to know who was going to be running the household. That is when I decided to actually spend "quality, quiet time" with Jesus and journaling became the central focus of my time. Through journaling I began writing love letters to God. It was during this time that I began clearly hearing Him speak to me. With my pen in hand I could feel the connection with my new Lord and Savior. This was the beginning of the most beautiful love relationship I had ever experienced.

Since that time, I have heard and seen the Lover of my soul through many facets of this life journey. But it is through writing that I have been able to discern and share His message with others. Two years ago my wonderful husband was diagnosed with Stage 3 colorectal cancer and I began sharing our miracle journey of healing through e-mail with our friends and family. I was determined to only write when it was God inspired. Throughout these e-mails I was encouraged to share my stories with others through the writing of this devotional book.

All of the stories are lessons our Lord and Savior taught me through various venues of my life. Some are from our cancer journey, some from my journey with *Courage to Teach*, and some from the mire and muck of everyday life. Each story is a simple message that God used to help me get to know Him better. As He used the simple happenings of everyday life to pull me out of the miry clay, He became my Rock and Lover of my soul. I pray Christ will use these stories to help "steady your feet and establish your goings." (Psalm 40:2)

In His precious love,

Susan

Broken Shells

When Billy and I got married we made a pact that we would celebrate each year of our marriage in a way that would continue to build memories to last a life time; we decided to celebrate each year with another "honeymoon." Our third year anniversary came right after Billy's cancer diagnosis and he was in the middle of his "chemo-radiation combo" treatment. Therefore, we decided we would wait until his rest and recover period to go on our "honeymoon" to Fort Morgan Alabama in the Gulf Shores. We love the beach and knew it would be the perfect time to allow God to heal and strengthen us for the next portion of His healing journey through surgery.

October came and finally we packed up the car with all our beach gear, our two dogs, George and Jake, along with *How Full is Your Bucket?* by Tom Rath and Donald Clifton (Great book I would recommend!) and headed for the Gulf Shores. Sitting on the snow white beach, Billy read to me and we had great discussions on bucket filling and bucket dipping. Boy, did God fill our buckets that week with His awesome creations.

We found huge shells on the beach—the size of Billy's hand. As I combed the beach each day looking for shells I realized how grateful I am that God doesn't look for us in the same manner . . . . you know, looking for the perfect shell with no holes, cracks or breaks. At this point, God opened my eyes to see the beauty in the brokenness of the shells. I began to see more character in the shells as I retrieved the broken ones to add to my collection. The really old ones had many pits/holes all over them and they were much thicker. Many of the huge shells that were in pieces looked like angels wings resting in the sand. The conch shells were so awesome and with each broken shell I could see even more of its intricate beauty in the inner structure. Now, God didn't stop there. He then opened my eyes to see not only the brokenness of the shell but to see the missing parts and to see just how beautiful the shell was created to be. I saw not just the outside but the wonderful detail of the inner structure that provided shelter and protection for various creatures.

Next, God gently reminded me that when I finally "washed up on shore" I too was very broken and empty. Yet He CHOSE me and saw me as He created me to be! He also reminded me that no matter how many times we get battered around and feel washed up, He will use our imperfections, holes, cracks or breaks and fill them with His marvelous light. AND, if we will just allow Him to fill us daily to overflow with His light, others will see Him in us and not the holes, cracks or breaks—they too will see the inner beauty and intricate structure that provides us shelter and protection through any and all storms—Jesus Christ! They too will see what God created us to be and then see what He created them to be!

³ You made all the delicate, inner parts of my body and knit me together in my mother's womb.
¹⁴ Thank you for making me so wonderfully complex! Your workmanship is marvelous—how well I know it.
¹⁵ You watched me as I was being formed in utter seclusion, as I was woven together in the dark of the womb. **Psalm 139:13-15** *(AMP)*

How has God filled your imperfections, holes, cracks or breaks?

_____

_____

_____

_____

_____

_____

What imperfections, holes, cracks or breaks do you still need filled?

_____

_____

_____

_____

_____

_____

What do you need to do to allow God to fill these imperfections, holes, cracks or breaks?

_____

_____

_____

_____

_____

_____

Chasing Crabs

Fort Morgan has become a very special retreat for all of us, Billy, George, Jake and me. God has truly used this special beach to teach me so many lessons. This particular time, He used "the boys" (George and Jake our dogs) along with the white sand crabs, which they just love to chase.

At night we would walk along the shore with a flashlight and laugh at the boys trying to catch the crabs. They would see one and chase it until it went into the ocean and then start looking for another. We would shine the light in front of them and try to help them see the small crabs. As soon as they would see one, they would take off pouncing on it and trying to grab it with their mouth. They would even dig down in the sand until all you could see was their little white tails wagging. They were truly enthralled with them and determined to catch one.

Many times we would see a crab, shine the light on it and call the boys. Since they knew our voices and trusted us, they would immediately turn and run toward where we were pointing. However, many times they would run right past the crab, thinking they saw something up ahead. This made me think about how God shines His light and points out just what it is He wants me to see. Like George and Jake, I see the light, hear His voice and go running toward it only to pass what He has in store because "I think I see what it is He has for me . . . only to find I missed it!"

Wanting to help the boys after they ran past the crab, we would call and flash the light to redirect them until either they found the crab or it scurried off out of sight. Isn't this what God does when I run past Him heading into the dark and miss what He has for me? It is amazing how patient and sovereign God is; He just keeps calling and flashing His light until I slow down, stop, listen and look back to Him to find the blessing He has for me.

Funny how this beach has become so special to us and how God has used it to remind us of His great love, mercy, grace and guidance! Just remember to keep listening to His call, looking for His light and above all keep Praising His Holy name. He so longs for you to find His blessings in His light.

²The man who enters by the gate is the shepherd of his sheep. ³The watchman opens the gate for him, and the sheep listen to his voice. He calls his own sheep by name and leads them out. ⁴When he has brought out all his own, he goes on ahead of them, and his sheep follow him because they know his voice.

John 10:2-4 (AMP)

What have you run to thinking it was what God had for you?

_____

_____

_____

_____

_____

_____

When did you realize you had missed what God was shining His light on for you?

_____

_____

_____

_____

_____

Where do you see God shining His light for you oday?

_____

_____

_____

_____

_____

What are you doing to make sure you don't run past it?

_____

_____

_____

_____

_____

_____

Lessons From "The Boys"

George and Jake, "the boys" are the only children we have left at home. They are our two dogs, a Jack Russell and a Parsons Russell. They have brought us so much joy and laughter as we have trained them to be our well behaved and totally spoiled children. Billy jokes that they have never known life without a king sized bed, air conditioning and a swimming pool. We have grown so attached to them that we seek "pet friendly" accommodations when we travel just so they can go with us. They absolutely love to go for a ride and visit new places with new smells.

Like most proud dog owners, we think our boys are so smart, cute and lovable. They not only know how to sit, lie down, stay, leave it and wait, they know how to spell. Yes, if you say "t r e a t" they will jump up, look excitedly at you, and take off to the kitchen expecting you to be right behind them and present them with some sort of treat. They even know how to make choices. If you present them with more than one treat and ask them which one they want, they will carefully sniff each choice and take the one they like the best. If you leave the cabinet open and their favorite chicken jerky is not a choice, they will snub all choices and look at you as if to say; "Uh, you forgot one!"

They have become so attached to us and have learned us so well that if we begin to pack a suitcase they become anxious, unless we reinforce to them that they are going with us. If we are packing the car for a trip and leave the door open, they will jump in and not get out ensuring they will not get left. They truly bring to life the old saying about "following you around like a puppy." When we leave them at home, they wait patiently in the bay window watching for our return. As soon as they hear us, they come running out of their doggy door, down the long, winding drive way only to have us stop to let them in the car to greet us. They greet us with tails wagging, mouths smiling and panting with excitement to just be with us once again. While they are six and seven years old now, they still long to be with us every minute of the day, even if it is just to curl up at our feet or in our laps and sleep. Each moment of each day is as if it is a totally new opportunity to love and be loved.

One day I was reflecting on the totally uninhibited, unconditional love the boys give to us each and every day and it made me realize that I should seek Jesus with the same longing, passion and love. Paul tells us to pray without ceasing. He tells us we should seek Jesus 24/7/365 and to do so with joy. Paul knew that if we are to build a true love relationship with Jesus then we have to spend time with Him and seek Him the same way a groom pursues his bride.

God used the boys to help me see that to pray without ceasing is to long to love and be loved by Jesus every moment of every day. It made me wonder what my relationship with Jesus would be like if I followed Him around like a "little puppy," even if it was just to curl up at His feet and rest. It made me wonder about my expressions each time I ran out my door to Jesus. Did I run smiling and panting with excitement to just be reunited with Him or did I only run to Him when I was frightened, sad or in trouble? Did I miss being in His presence and seek Him out like the boys do us? Do I study His every move and try to learn His ways so I can be with Him each step of the way? When He is ready to take me to new places, do I run and get in with the anticipation and excitement of the new adventure or do I lag behind wanting to stay in my comfort zone? Do I see Him running down the long winding driveway begging me to open the door and let Him in way before I reach my destination? Oh, how I long to be like the boys and lavish my love on Jesus 24/7/365. All the distractions of this world make it difficult to achieve, but the boys are a constant reminder of how I should be seeking Jesus!

"16Be happy [in your faith] and rejoice and be glad-hearted continually (always);
17Be unceasing in prayer [praying perseveringly];
18Thank [God] in everything [no matter what the circumstances may be, be thankful and give thanks], for this is the will of God for you [who are] in Christ Jesus [the Revealer and Mediator of that will]."
1 Thessalonians 5:16-18 (AMP)

How do you create new opportunities to love and be loved by Jesus?

_____

_____

_____

_____

_____

_____

When was last time you curled up at Jesus' feet to rest?

_____

_____

_____

_____

_____

What do you need to do to slow down to let Jesus come along?

_____

_____

_____

_____

_____

Loving the Unlovable

When Billy and I got married I had a cat, Buckwheat, who had been with me for a very long time. She was given to me after my first divorce and she had endured all of the ups and downs of my life before, during, and after letting Christ out of my guest room. While Buckwheat was not the cuddling type of cat, she was the one constant in my life and I was very attached to her.

After marrying Billy and moving into our new home, she was given the run of the upstairs. Since she was 18 years old at the time and would not tolerate dogs, we put a baby gate up on the landing to the upstairs so the boys could not get to her. While this worked well for about a year, one day Jake got a "run and go" and jumped over the railing and got to her. Despite our attempt to take her to the emergency room, she did not make it.

This event marks one of the most difficult times in my life. You see, I not only grieved the loss of such a constant companion, I had to see Jake every day. Each time I would see him, I was reminded of the horrible death Buckwheat had to endure. While I knew her health was failing and she was becoming more and more fragile each day, I never wanted her to experience such a violent death.

Jake was only doing what a Parson Russell was bred to do. How could I hold it against him? He didn't know he had done anything wrong. Each day he would come up to me numerous times with his tail wagging, smiling and panting and wanting to comfort his sad, crying owner. Each time I would try to pet him I would be consumed with grief, anger and hurt. Here was this cute, adorable, loving dog trying to cheer me up but I struggled to move forward. I knew I had to get past this or get rid of Jake.

Then one day, I was reminded of the grace and mercy God showed me. I knew God was calling me to love the unlovable just as He loved us. I knew God was calling me to forgive my dog and to show him the same unconditional love God showed me. I wondered how I was ever going to be able to look at Jake and not replay that horrible scene in my mind. Then God led me to Lamentations 3:22-24 which says that God's mercy, loving-kindness, and compassion are NEW EVERY MORNING!

He reminded me that our slate is wiped clean each and every day and I was called to do the same . . . with ALL of His creation! He also told me through this scripture that "we are not consumed, BECAUSE His compassions fail not!" He was telling me that if I would just allow Him to fill me, He would heal my hurt and take away my anger and turn my sorrow into joy. HE would give me His love, compassion, grace and mercy to share with Jake. I didn't have to rely on mine.

After this, every time Jake would come to me, I would ask God to help me to show him His compassion, grace, mercy and love. At first, I would cry through each prayer and force myself to reach out in God's love to Jake. After a while, I was able to do this without crying and before you knew it, God was lavishing His love all over me through Jake once more.

As a school teacher, I have learned to practice wiping the slate clean each and every day my students enter my room. I tell them that God did it for me and I was called to do it for them. So no matter how bad of a day I may have with a challenging student, the next day I greet them at the door with a smile and expectations of having a great day. While I still cry when I remember the horrible scene that day with Jake, God has truly turned my sorrow into joy as Jake has brought me many days filled with laughter, love and joy, as have many challenging students! God used my pets to teach me how sweet love is when it is given through His compassions and forgiveness.

²²It is because of the Lord's mercy and loving-kindness that we are not consumed, because His [tender] compassions fail not.⁽ᴬ⁾
²³They are new every morning; great and abundant is Your stability and faithfulness.⁽ᴮ⁾
²⁴The Lord is my portion or share, says my living being (my inner self); therefore will I hope in Him and wait expectantly for Him.⁽ᶜ⁾

Lamentations 3:22-24 (AMP)

Who in your life do you need to forgive and show them you love them?

_____

_____

_____

_____

_____

_____

What are you still holding on to that God has wiped clean?

_____

_____

_____

_____

_____

Who is God using in your life to show you His unconditional love? How is He using them?

_____

_____

_____

_____

_____

Root Bound

Billy and I both love plants and love to watch them grow. The entryway to our home we turned into a sunroom that looks more like a solarium. It has a small gate leg table with two chairs that barely fit in the room due to the number of plants. It is not quite as crowded in the spring and summer because we take half of the plants outside. However, in the fall and winter when it is time to move the plants inside, the room begins to look like a jungle.

In the winter, you will find us in this jungle having many of our meals at the small table. Our favorite meal in the jungle is on Saturday morning enjoying a long lazy breakfast. As we drink our coffee, we discuss the plants and how they are doing. Some of them die back and look as if they will not come back; but, we keep watering and nurturing them because we know in the spring they will grow and blossom once again. Other plants continue to flourish in the warmth and sunshine the room provides with the floor to ceiling wall of windows. Our Christmas cactus loves this room and provides us the beautiful Christmas blooms on and off all year long.

It is during these long lazy morning plant inspections that we will notice plants that have become root bound. While these plants still look great and could continue to look the same if left alone, we realize they will not reach their potential because the roots have no more room to grow. We know it is time to get a bigger pot, new soil, aerate the roots, and repot the plant if we are going to see it become what God created it to be.

One day I noticed a plant that was spilling over the pot and looking just beautiful; however, upon further inspection I could see it was getting root bound. During the quiet of the moment, God opened my eyes to understand that my spiritual life was like this plant. I had been growing and flourishing in the same pot for quite a while. On the outside of the pot, I still looked green, fresh and had blooms. Nevertheless, under the soil and inside the pot, my roots had grown all they could grow with the space the pot provided.

God was showing me that it was time I move to a bigger pot; it was time for new soil; it was time I grow deeper in my relationship with Him. But, I was comfortable in this old pot and besides, I was still blooming. Was it really necessary that I move? What if I don't like the new pot and began to wilt? What will happen to the old pot? Will I lose my blooms; will I be hurt?

John tells us that God prunes those who bear fruit so they will grow bigger, better and more fruit. I knew I had to trust our Heavenly Father as the ultimate gardener and allow him to repot me. I knew if I was ever going to become who God created me to be that I needed new soil, my roots aerated and a bigger pot. The new soil became a deeper type of devotional time . . . reading about God from other people was not enough, I had to get into His word from Him. Aerating my roots meant I had to shed the baggage . . . I had to release the hurt and anger through forgiveness of others. The bigger pot meant I had to expand my territory . . . I had to get involved in more than just going to church; I had to get involved in serving God through my church.

Like the plant we repotted, at first I wilted a little as I struggled to get use to my new environment. But once my roots got settled, they began to grow again and it felt so good to be growing in new ways. I began to see that God has more planned for me; that He created me to be more than I was in the old pot. Yes, He is stretching me and sometimes it is uncomfortable. But let me tell you, the new fruit is bigger, better and much more than I had ever dreamed.

How are your roots? Do they have room to grow or do you need a bigger new pot? If so, trust your Heavenly Father to gently lift you out, aerate your roots, provide you new soil and place you gently into a new pot where He already knows you will flourish.

[1] "I am the true vine, and my Father is the gardener. [2] He cuts off every branch in me that bears no fruit, while every branch that does bear fruit he prunes[a] so that it will be even more fruitful.

John 15: 1 (AMP)

What type of new soil does your spiritual life need?

_____

_____

_____

_____

_____

_____

What will it take to aerate your roots to stimulate them to grow deeper in Christ?

_____

_____

_____

_____

_____

What does your new pot look like?

_____

_____

_____

_____

_____

Score Another for God

Have you ever gone on the much needed vacation only to step into the beginnings of what you thought to be either a nightmare or some really sick twisted comedy where you were the brunt of all the jokes? Well, right after Billy was diagnosed with Stage 3 colorectal cancer we took our first trip to the Gulf Shores in Alabama and satan tried real hard to turn this trip into just that, a nightmare or sick twisted comedy. Satan took the ball and was running straight for the goal line from the time we arrived and he thought he was about to score big.

Upon our arrival to the condo, it was obviously not ready for new guest as the beds were still stripped of the sheets and comforters. Next we locked the boys, George and Jake (our dogs) in the condo by accident when we went down to the car to get all of our luggage. I called the owner of the condo who lived in Birmingham, Alabama. She had told the cleaning lady the wrong day of our arrival and scheduled her to come the next day. She then called her sister who lived at Gulf Shores, to come immediately to let us back in the condo, provide fresh towels and to put new sheets on the beds. All of this, only to discover her sister was on her way back from Austin, TX and was in Biloxi, two hours away.

Satan was off and running . . . he's at the 30, 40, and now 50 yard line when suddenly he goes down hard. Tackled by the owner and the cleaning lady who had been praying for us. You see, the owner of the condo was aware of our situation and had told the cleaning lady and both had been praying for us. Also, the owner told us we were "so getting our security deposit and cleaning fee all back!" We decided to go out to eat while we waited on her sister to arrive with a key. We had a nice relaxing meal and were able to laugh at the situation. It's amazing how things like this seemed so small in comparison to the big picture, Stage 3 Colorectal cancer.

Once we were settled in the condo, we enjoyed our evening relaxing in front of the TV. However it was first and ten on the 50 yard line and satan was back up and running. Friday the air conditioning was not working properly. It was July at the Gulf Shores and heat was rising in the condo. Once again, I called the owner who immediately called the AC guy. The AC guy now was told about Billy's cancer and He took satan down behind the line of scrimmage. He was not only praying but told us to look up 2 Chronicles 16:8.

The air seemed to be fixed and we were still keeping it all in perspective and allowing God to provide us with the rest and strength we would need for this cancer journey. It was now third and twenty for satan but he was able to get away running again. The air went out again! At this point the owner got the air fixed and also offered for us to return in November or December when Billy was at a point in treatments/surgeries he felt like traveling. She also asked if I would please keep her updated on Billy so she could continue to pray and keep others updated.

Score! He's in the end zone . . . wait, he is in the end zone, but it is the wrong end zone. Satan was off and running but got turned around and ran to the wrong end zone and scored another one for our Lord and Savior! We loved our visit to the Gulf Shores and knew we would return. It was on this trip we discovered Fort Morgan Beach and have been back every year since. What started out as a nightmare or bad comedy turned into huge blessings around each mishap.

It was absolutely incredible to watch as God totally destroyed satan each time he tried to steal our joy. It was amazing how God had gone before us in prayer through strangers and protected us each step of the way. While satan was trying to steal our joy, God was adding more and more people in the Body of Christ to be lifting us up in prayer.

WOW ISN'T OUR GOD GREAT! Oh, the power of the Body of Christ . . . . there have been so many people we do not even know who are praying for us; and let me tell you, we sure felt it. This vacation was the beginning of God filling us with such a peace that covered us each step of the way and it was being sent to us through the Body of Christ as so many people prayed for us. Next time you find yourself in a nightmare or a bad comedy, read 2 Chronicles 16:8 and just sit back and watch another score for God.

8 Were not the Cushites [a] and Libyans a mighty army with great numbers of chariots and horsemen [b]? Yet when you relied on the LORD, he delivered them into your hand. 9 For the eyes of the LORD range throughout the earth to strengthen those whose hearts are fully committed to him.

2 Chronicles 16:8 *(AMP)*

Where in your life do you feel satan has the ball and is off and running?

_____

_____

_____

_____

_____

_____

What scripture reminds you that satan is running toward the wrong goal?

_____

_____

_____

_____

_____

_____

Who has God put in your life to remind you, or how has God used you to remind others, that satan just scored another one for God?

_____

_____

_____

_____

_____

_____

Candy Along the Way

The pleasures of riding a bicycle come early in life. It begins when you take that first ride without the training wheels. That ride where a parent holds the back of the bike to help you get your balance before taking off. That ride where a parent runs along beside you to ensure your safety as you learn to maintain your balance and speed. As your skills and confidence builds, you learn to displace the challenge of the ride with the pleasure and joy of the ride.

The pleasure and joy that comes with the feel of the wind in your face as you roll along taking in all of the scenery is what continues to propel Billy and I to mount up and hit the road in search of the best scenery with the least number of hills. One particular morning, we rose early and headed over the mountain to Walker County, Georgia to do what we now call the "Hog Jowl Road ride." Billy had used Google Earth to help him discover this beautiful 30 mile loop ride. While most of the ride is fairly easy rolling hills, we discovered the hardest hills were toward the end of the ride.

Since this was my first ride of any length in a long time, after 20 miles my energy began to wane, my legs became weak and my breathing labored more and more as we climbed each hill. As we stopped at the top of a long hill, Billy gave me some candy he had packed in his bike bag. He told me it helped him to keep going when he got tired. I popped the first piece into my mouth and off we went to tackle the next hill. As the candy began to melt in my mouth, I began to focus on the sweet taste of the candy instead of the ache and burn in my legs.

The sweetness of the candy helped me to shift my focus off of the challenge of the hills back to the pleasure and joy of the ride. With each new hill, came a new piece of candy along with a prayer for strength to finish the ride. The combination of candy and prayer to help me overtake each hill made me think about how God places "candy" in our lives to help us shift our focus off of our problems and challenges. Many times the "candy" is found in scripture, through devotion or song, or a call or visit from a friend or family member.

Many of our journeys in life start off like the "Hog Jowl Road Ride" where you find yourself on a road you have never seen. At first, the beauty and mystery of what lies ahead keeps you going. However, eventually the stress of the hills takes its toll and you begin wondering if the ride will ever smooth out again. The "candy" God provides, becomes a gentle reminder that when we face the hills and mountains in life, our energy and strength will be renewed if we will just savor the sweetness of HIs "candy."

[28] Do you not know? Have you not heard? The LORD is the everlasting God, the Creator of the ends of the earth. He will not grow tired or weary, and his understanding

no one can fathom. [29] He gives strength to the weary and increases the power of the weak. [30] Even youths grow tired and weary, and young men stumble and fall; [31] but those who hope in the LORD will renew their strength. They will soar on wings like eagles; they will run and not grow weary, they will walk and not be faint.

Isaiah 40: 28-32 (AMP)

What candy has God provided you in your journey?

_____

_____

_____

_____

_____

_____

_____

What candy do you need to taste now to help you refocus on the pleasure and joy?

_____

_____

_____

_____

_____

_____

Who in your life can you share your candy to help their ride become smoother or provide them an energy boost?

_____

_____

_____

_____

_____

_____

Flowers from Fertilizer

My "BCR" (Before Christ Ruled) days are not days I long to remember as they were filled with selfish ways of prideful indulgence and sin. Needless to say, I made a lot of very bad decisions that led to a lot of very bad mistakes. Even after I allowed Christ out of the guest room, I carried around this bag of horrible memories and shame for quite a while. It was on my Walk to Emmaus, a spiritual retreat, which I finally realized that this bag was getting in between me and Jesus and something had to go. It was at the foot of the cross that I was able to lay this bag down and leave it.

Without the cumbersome size and weight of that bag of shame, I was free to take the next steps in my relationship with Christ. Through Christ's grace, love and mercy my shame was washed away and He was able to use my past to help others. I met people and taught students who were going through or facing the same decisions I packed in that bag and left at the cross. The more I turned my life over to Christ, the more people He put in my path that needed to know about His grace, love and mercy.

A colleague I met in a prayer group who was facing divorce came to me because she remembered I had been there. Christ used my experience to help protect and guide her through this hurtful part of her life. Students were drawn to me because they knew I would not judge them; I simply loved them for who they were, where there were. Besides, who was I to judge anyone with my past? I was astonished at how my sinful past was being used to open doors for me to share how Christ healed me and made me whole.

I never would have guessed that when I laid that bag down, Christ would use it. Like fertilizer spread on a flower garden, my past became fertile soil to grow beautiful flowers for Christ. Ask.com defines fertilizer as: "Any of a large number of natural and synthetic materials, including manure and nitrogen, phosphorus, and potassium compounds, spread on or worked into soil to increase its capacity to support plant growth." The natural and synthetic materials in my bag were infused with Christ's grace, mercy and love and now Christ was working it into my soil to increase my capacity to support spiritual growth in others!

When Billy was diagnosed with cancer, God called me to share that journey with others. As God guided my hand to write, so many people responded about the blessing they had received from each update. Again, Christ was using the fertilizer in our life to increase our capacity to support spiritual growth. As we shared how God was sustaining us through this journey, He used this horrible disease and time of suffering to once again grow beautiful flowers.

Then one day, God opened my eyes to 2 Corinthians 1: 3-7 to help me to see that we are not only to call on Him and realize His strength, compassion and comfort in our times of struggle, mistakes and suffering but that He gives this to us as a gift to share with others. The strength, compassion, and comfort are ours "SO THAT we can comfort those in any trouble . . ." Wow, the grace, mercy and love Christ used to wash away my mistakes and shame along with His gifts of strength, compassion and comfort have been "spread on and worked into" my soul to help grow His beautiful garden. Amazingly enough, the fertilizer of my life was being used by Christ to grow beautiful flowers!

³Praise be to the God and Father of our Lord Jesus Christ, the Father of compassion and the God of all comfort, ⁴who comforts us in all our troubles, so that we can comfort those in any trouble with the comfort we ourselves have received from God. ⁵For just as the sufferings of Christ flow over into our lives, so also through Christ our comfort overflows. ⁶If we are distressed, it is for your comfort and salvation; if we are comforted, it is for your comfort, which produces in you patient endurance of the same sufferings we suffer. ⁷And our hope for you is firm, because we know that just as you share in our sufferings, so also you share in our comfort.

2 Corinthians 1: 3-7 (AMP)

Who has Christ put in your life so you could share your story of grace and mercy?

_____

_____

_____

_____

_____

_____

How is Christ turning your fertilizer into flowers?

_____

_____

_____

_____

_____

Where is Christ calling you to use your fertilizer to increase your capacity to support others spiritual growth?

_____

_____

_____

_____

_____

I Want One of Those!

One of the flowers God grew out of my fertilizer was being able to understand the deep longing and desire women have for their prince to take them into "happily ever after" and how this desire can create impatience and poor decisions. While I have shared this story with many single women, the most precious was recently when my step-daughter came home after breaking up with her long-time boyfriend. Although she knew it was the right thing to do, the hurt and fear was compounded with the future days of being alone.

As we sat on the back porch, she shared the details of the breakup and her fears of being alone. I then shared with her how I would go to Emmaus gatherings and hear husbands introduce themselves and their wives. During this introduction the husband would always say something like: "I worship and serve our Risen Lord and Savior at whatever church along with my beautiful, loving and caring wife." I would just sit there and say to myself: "I want one of those!" I so longed and desired to have a Christian husband who would love God and me in that way. I had such a huge hole in my heart from this empty desire and it just seemed to rule my life.

One night as I was home alone in the bathroom, I was engulfed by the emptiness of this desire. I sank down the wall and just sobbed and cried out to God. I asked him to please either fill it or take it away from me. I hated what it was doing to me and I just wanted it to go away. Well, God did fill it, but only part of it. He got me so involved in allowing Him to be the lover of my soul that the emptiness began to go away.

God began to lavish His love on me as I became more involved through serving Him. I became a youth counselor at our church. I began taking the Disciple classes at our church. After running the slides for the songs during our contemporary service, I was asked to sing with the praise team. Boy did God fill the void in my life as He poured out His love all over me. Whenever anyone would ask if I was dating someone, I would tell them "yes, I was deeply in love with Jesus and He kept me very busy!"

Then one day I realized that He had NOT filled the entire hole. The desire for that Christian husband was still there. At first I was fearful of being engulfed by the emptiness again, but then I realized that the hole that was left was His promise to me. This was his promise; this was my hope! Now that I was delighting myself in God through serving Him with all my heart, soul and strength, He allowed me to see the hole was still there. He was showing me His promise. You see, God would never give us a desire He would not fill.

God did give me that desire and then some. He blessed me with the most wonderful, loving, gentle, kind and compassionate Christian husband! I now "have one of those!" So, if you have a hole of emptiness in your life, release it to God and He will fill it. Just be aware that how He fills it may not be what you think. But He promises that if you:

⁴Delight yourself also in the Lord, and He will give you the desires and secret petitions of your heart. ⁵Commit your way to the Lord [roll and repose each care of your load on Him]; trust (lean on, rely on, and be confident) also in Him and He will bring it to pass.

Psalm 37: 4-5 (AMP)

What longing desire do you need to commit to God

_____

_____

_____

_____

_____

_____

How do you "delight yourself in the Lord?"

_____

_____

_____

_____

_____

_____

In what ways do you need to allow God to pour out His love all over you?

_____

_____

_____

_____

_____

_____

Covered in Feathers

I have never been the type of person who picks ups items just because I found them. I need to have a purpose for it if I am going to pick it up and carry it home. Even shells on the beach—I will not just collect them without a specific purpose for them when I get home. My family lovingly and jokingly calls my dad "Mr. Clean" and my mother tells me that "I am my father's child." So, I guess you could say I come by this trait honestly.

There is only one time in my life that caused me to start "collecting" something that didn't have a specific purpose. One day I was walking along the beach at Jekyll Island listening to my Christian music in deep, prayerful thought. I had really been struggling with a personal situation. I needed to make a tough decision and I was so afraid I would mess up again. I so did not want to go back to the old life; so, during this walk I was seeking to gain some understanding, guidance and peace.

As I walked I saw numerous shells and other remnants of ocean life washed up on the shore. While I may have slowed my pace or even stopped to pick it up and look at it, I would put it back and continue on with my walk. Then all of a sudden I saw a large white feather lying up ahead. I stopped, picked it up and studied the feather for a few moments. As I was about to place it back on the ground, I felt God was telling me: "Not this one. Hold on to it. Take it home."

As per usual, I wrestled with God and wanted to know why I should take this feather home. What was I going to do with it? Where would I put it? Come on, a feather? I continued to feel God telling me to take it home and He would show me. So, I carried the feather back to the apartment, packed it in my suitcase, carried it home, and walked around the house trying to figure out where to put this feather. Finally, I decided I would put it in my devotional basket.

The feather sat in the basket for two to three days before God revealed to me His purpose. One morning as I was reading my Women of Destiny Devotional Bible, I was lead to a full page devotional based on Psalm 91. There it was! The reason God had me bring the feather home. He was telling me that as long as I stay with Him, He would take care of me. The feather was His promise that He has me covered at all times and I don't need to worry about going back to that old life. I could trust in Him to carry me through any and all tough decisions.

Since that day, I continue to pick up every feather God places in my path. One day a friend called me all upset and needing to talk. As I arrived at her house, I found a feather in her front yard. I picked it up and took it in with me. Before I left, I gave her the feather and told her to look up Psalm 91. The next day she thanked me for leading her to such a wonderful message from God.

I now saw my purpose in picking up feathers. So, I created a beautiful graphic of a feather floating down onto the beach along with the Psalm 91:4 scripture. I then punched holes to place a feather through the graphic to give to friends in need. I even have this most horrendous arrangement I made from about 50 feathers that I had found. It sits in my den on my coffee table. Each time I look at it I am reminded of Gods promise. Then I am reminded of how ugly this arrangement is and am tempted to throw it out. However, there is just something in me that won't allow me to do that.

I continue to find feathers along my faith journey and it is amazing how each time I find them they seem to come at such an appropriate time. Either to share with someone in need or to remind me that like a chick under its mother's wings, God has me covered, protected, and secured under His almighty wing!

[1]He who [a]dwells in the secret place of the Most High shall remain stable and fixed under the shadow of the Almighty [Whose power no foe can withstand]. [2]I will say of the Lord, He is my Refuge and my Fortress, my God; on Him I lean and rely, and in Him I [confidently] trust! [3]For [then] He will deliver you from the snare of the fowler and from the deadly pestilence. [4][Then] He will cover you with His pinions, and under His wings shall you trust and find refuge; His truth and His faithfulness

are a shield and a buckler. [5]You shall not be afraid of the terror of the night, nor of the arrow (the evil plots and slanders of the wicked) that flies by day, [6]Nor of the pestilence that stalks in darkness, nor of the destruction and sudden death that surprise and lay waste at noonday. [7]A thousand may fall at your side, and ten thousand at your right hand, but it shall not come near you. [8]Only a spectator shall you be [yourself inaccessible in the secret place of the Most High] as you witness the reward of the wicked. [9]Because you have made the Lord your refuge, and the Most High your dwelling place,[(A)] [10]There shall no evil befall you, nor any plague or calamity come near your tent. [11]For He will give His angels [especial] charge over you to accompany and defend and preserve you in all your ways [of obedience and service]. [12]They shall bear you up on their hands, lest you dash your foot against a stone.[(B)] [13]You shall tread upon the lion and adder; the young lion and the serpent shall you trample underfoot. [(C)] [14]Because he has set his love upon Me, therefore will I deliver him; I will set him on high, because he knows and understands My name [has a personal knowledge of My mercy, love, and kindness—trusts and relies on Me, knowing I will never forsake him, no, never]. [15]He shall call upon Me, and I will answer him; I will be with him in trouble, I will deliver him and honor him. [16]With long life will I satisfy him and show him My salvation.
Psalm 91 (AMP)

Dead Trees and Deep Roots

The years of 2004 and 2005 brought me many blessings along with deep growth. One of these blessings came when I was asked to be part of the Courage to Teach (CTT) Program. This program consists of four retreats each year, one retreat each season. During these retreats we would work together through large group discussions, small group sharing and individual reflection time designed to help us "reconnect with what keeps us feeling alive and whole in our life and work." We were provided various readings along with open-ended, deep, thought provoking questions to "deepen our own inner journey and nurture new possibilities for our work in education." (No, this is not a cult! ☺)

God placed me with an incredible group of women who were most all Christians. Needless to say, these "educational retreats" turned into to spiritual retreats for most of us. God used the readings to help me connect my spiritual journey with His creation of the seasons. The one season that stood out the most to me was winter and how it connects to spiritual journeys through the desert. During my individual reflection time, I took a long walk through the woods observing and studying what winter looks and feels like.

The tree's branches were leafless and bare; but, the trunk looked the same as in the other seasons. All of this was nothing new to me. However, it is what I couldn't see below the earth's surface that stopped me in my tracks. It was what was happening beneath the leaf laden ground that spoke to me the most. For the first time I was gaining a deeper understanding of how God used this time of dormancy to provide the tree with what it would need to grow, bloom and prosper.

If the tree tried to hold on to its leaves during this time, there would not be enough nutrients to sustain the growth of the tree and it would die trying to keep the leaves alive. So, God uses the old rotten leaves to provide the sustaining nutrients of the rich winter soil. What looks like mire and muck around the tree as the dirt, water and leaves meld together, turns out to be how the tree utilizes what God equipped it with for nourishment and warmth during these cold, long, dark winter months. At the same time, the new foliage in the spring is the direct results of the sustaining nutrient the old leaves provide during this time of dormancy.

It is also during this time that the roots grow deeper as they search for nutrients to sustain life above ground. It is because of this deep root growth that the tree does not fall over during high winds and storms. You see, if the roots are always given what they need at a shallow point in the soil, they would never have to seek nutrients; therefore, they would easily be pulled from the soil during high winds and storms or even by the weight of its own trunk and branches. So while above the earth the tree looks ugly and dead, deep within the soil there is growth that will keep the tree standing firm and tall.

By the end of my walk God presented me numerous new deep, thought provoking questions which I continue to ponder to this day . . . What old leaves do I need to shed to allow God to meld with His living waters so that I may continue to grow in Christ? What leaves am I trying to keep alive that are causing other parts of me to die? Am I embracing the dormancy of my spiritual journey so my roots can grow deeper or am I just skimming the surface looking for any type of sustenance? During my winters, am I focusing on the cold bare branches above or the nutrients God is providing below the surface? Am I like the trunk and being faithful and steadfast to the roots no matter what it looks like on the outside or what the weather is around me? Am I allowing God the time and space to work in me or am I rushing winter with premature warmth that will not last me through the entire spring and summer? When I look in the mirror do I see the dormant tree or the life sustaining roots of who God created me to be?

These questions from my long winter walk have helped me to have faith that when life seems barren and empty this is when God is working the most to provide nourishment and deep growth so the spring will bring bright, full, beautiful flowers and foliage that will last. It truly is when we die to self and allow Christ to live in and through us that we become the most alive!

A Time for Everything

¹ There is a time for everything, and a season for every activity under heaven:

² a time to be born and a time to die, a time to plant and a time to uproot,

³ a time to kill and a time to heal, a time to tear down and a time to build,

⁴ a time to weep and a time to laugh, a time to mourn and a time to dance,

⁵ a time to scatter stones and a time to gather them, a time to embrace and a time to refrain, ⁶ a time to search and a time to give up, a time to keep and a time to throw away, a time to tear and a time to mend, a time to be silent and a time to speak, ⁸ a time to love and a time to hate, a time for war and a time for peace.

⁹ What does the worker gain from his toil? ¹⁰ I have seen the burden God has laid on men. ¹¹ He has made everything beautiful in its time.

Ecclesiastes 3: 1-11 (AMP)

What nourishment has God provided for you during your "dormant" winter?

_____

_____

_____

_____

_____

_____

What have you tried to hold on to that held you back from growing?

_____

_____

_____

_____

_____

_____

What new growth was a result of the dormant winter?

_____

_____

_____

_____

_____

_____

Dance With Me

God has used many venues in my life to speak to me. He has used scripture, circumstances, friends, family, and music. However, there have been a few precious occasions where I could hear Him speaking directly to me. On this particular day, I was out running and God chose this time to give me the words to begin to write my faith journey. I became so focused on listening to Him that I finished running my route in what seemed like no time. As soon as I got home, I penned what God had given me, not knowing at the time it was only the first half. It was about a year later during my quiet time when He gave me the second half. Now I would like to share with you "Dance With Me—My Faith Journey:"

God said "dance with me.
Just take my hand;
I'll lead.
Close your eyes; now focus on Me.
I'll show you how; here, stand on My feet."

~

I listened to His words and tried to see His face.
I felt His arms surround me
I felt His love and grace.

~

He began to move me

I gripped a little tighter.
He whispered softly to me
"My child, I'll never leave you."
He waltzed me through the storms of life.
His mercy moved me gently.
He taught me how to trust Him and how to let Him lead.

~

I listened to His words and focused on His face.
I could feel His arms around me
I could feel His love and grace

~

He taught me all the steps.
My feet became much lighter.
Unsure of myself
I opened my eyes . . . .
. . . still in His arms, no longer on His feet.
Now on my own,
I danced with God,
In His timing, His rhythm, to His beat

~

I still listened to His words and focused on His face.
His arms were still around me as I danced in His love and
grace.

~

Now "rest a moment . . . .
Shhhh . . . my child"
He gently asked of me.
My precious, dancing child, just rest a while with me.

~

I listened to His words and focused on His face

I felt Him still the motion as He focused on my face.

Let me show you who you are.
Who I made you to be.
No matter where you go or where you've been,
MY child you'll always be.

I listened to His words as tears streamed down my face.
I felt Him lift the veil . . . .
. . . my guilt, my shame with His grace.

He showed me who I was though hard for me to see.
He showed me through His blood,
His daughter of grace . . .
. . . . was ME!

I listened to His words and focused on His face
I could feel His arms around me
I could feel His love and grace.

He holds me through the night.
He holds me through the day.
He looks me in the eyes and asks me just to stay.

I listen to His words and focus on His face.
I feel His calming spirit as I try to still my pace.

I wonder what is next.
He just holds me tight.
I wonder what to "do."

"Shhh . . . . not tonight . . . .
. . . . wait on me my child you'll see.
Just watch and listen and look for me . . . ."

¹*I WILL extol You, O Lord, for You have lifted me up and have not let my foes rejoice over me.* ²*O Lord my God, I cried to You and You have healed me.* ³*O Lord, You have brought my life up from Sheol (the place of the dead); You have kept me alive, that I should not go down to the pit (the grave).* ⁴*Sing to the Lord, O you saints of His, and give thanks at the remembrance of His holy name.* ⁵*For His anger is but for a moment, but His favor is for a lifetime or in His favor is life. Weeping may endure for a night, but joy comes in the morning.*⁽ᴬ⁾ ⁶*As for me, in my prosperity I said, I shall never be moved.* ⁷*By Your favor, O Lord, You have established me as a strong mountain; You hid Your face, and I was troubled.* ⁸*I cried to You, O Lord, and to the Lord I made supplication.* ⁹*What profit is there in my blood, when I go down to the pit (the grave)? Will the dust praise You? Will it declare Your truth and faithfulness to men?* ¹⁰*Hear, O Lord, have mercy and be gracious to me! O Lord, be my helper!* ¹¹*You have turned my mourning into dancing for me; You have put off my sackcloth and girded me with gladness,* ¹²*To the end that my tongue and my heart and everything glorious within me may sing praise to You and not be silent. O Lord my God, I will give thanks to You forever.*

Psalm 30 (AMP)

What events would comprise your faith journey?

_____

_____

_____

_____

_____

_____

What analogy would help you describe your faith journey?

_____

_____

_____

_____

_____

_____

How can God use this analogy to help you to wait on Him?

_____

_____

_____

_____

_____

_____

Foresight

I'm sure we have all had the conversation of how men and women are so very different. Not just their physical make up but how differently they do things and even think. We women like to boast about our multitasking and foresight all the time. We become convinced that when it comes to these two traits we have the corner on the market. I too thought this until we began Billy's cancer journey. That is when I realized what little foresight we have compared to God.

It began with doing the yard, cutting grass, weed eating, hedging, etc. Billy and I had many conversations over the amount of time it took to do the acres of yard where we live. He would spend at least two to three days doing yard work in the summer and I thought he needed this time to do other things, like riding his bike, gardening, and renovating our house. Finally, I had convinced him to hire our neighbor's son for the summer. It would free Billy up and provide this young man with his first summer job. What we didn't know, but God knew, was that the chemo and radiation would zap all of his energy and he would not feel like doing yard work. Also, it would increase his sensitivity to the sun and he would not be allowed out in the sun during this time. Wow, God used a nagging wife and a teenager in need of a job to go before us to provide a way to do yard work!

I was scheduled to present at a conference in Atlanta on Tuesday, July 22, 2008. Prior to the conference I e-mailed my PowerPoint presentation and notes to the person who was in charge of the project. She was going to put it on the laptop I would be using for the presentation to ensure it would run properly when I got there. While I was preparing the e-mail, I had a strong feeling that I should also copy the e-mail to my state supervisor, who served on the project team and I knew would be at the presentation. I wasn't sure why I needed to do this, so I jokingly told him that I did this in case something happened to me and he could wing it.

I can now hear God saying: "Oh my child if you only knew . . . but I got you covered." You see, Billy was diagnosed on Friday, July 18, 2008. Needless to say, we arrived at the conference on July 19 shaken to the core. God moved mountains to get Billy in to see a surgical oncologist that very next Monday at 2:00, July 21. We were approximately two hours away and could easily make it. I immediately sought out the project supervisor along with my state supervisor and explained the situation. It turned out that it was not a problem, since they both had the presentation prior to the conference and had time to become familiar with it. At that moment I knew it was God who had me copy my state supervisor on the e-mail and it was God who prepared them to give the presentation!

Next, we discovered how God had placed us with the best colorectal surgical oncologist in our area. After Billy's colonoscopy and the shocking diagnosis that they found a "malignant tumor," I called some friends who arrived at the surgical center to be with us right after Billy woke up. They arrived in time to be with us when the doctor was explaining to us the next steps. The doctor asked us if we knew a surgical oncologist. I didn't even know there was such a specialized doctor much less the name of one. At this point, our friend stepped out into the hall and began asking the nurses who they would recommend. They told him Dr. Portera, Jr. is who they would use. So that is the name we gave the doctor, and he said he would have his nurse see if she could get us in to see him.

It was nothing short of a miracle that there was a cancellation that left an opening that Monday at 2:00—Thank You Jesus! As we began the marathon of doctor appointments, consultations and tests, nurses and people began to ask us how in the world we were able to get Dr. Portera, Jr. as he stayed booked all the time. We then discovered that Dr. Portera, Jr. was known as the best surgical oncologist in our area. How did we get him? By God placing our friends at the surgical center fast enough to step in and have clear thinking to leave the room and ask the nurses. By God placing the right nurses in our friend's path when he went searching to find us a name. By God knowing there would be a cancellation that would allow us to get in immediately with Dr. Portera, Jr.

God had gone before us in so many ways and we were beginning to realize some of those ways. About a year prior to Billy's diagnosis, Neal, the husband of my sister's friend, who I did not know, was battling leukemia. My sister had asked me to pray for Neal and his family. Neal's wife, Lisa, was very diligent in keeping their Caring Bridge Web Page updated and I would faithfully read it. She used this venue to not only tell about Neal's condition but to witness how God was walking with them through this valley. She always included scriptures that God had given to them to comfort and guide them. I began to share Neal's story with my church family and we all prayed for them.

Many times I questioned why God had placed Neal so heavy on my heart and why I had gotten so involved. Here was this family I had never met and didn't even know, yet I cried and rejoiced for and with them though their long battle. Shortly after Neal's battle ended we began our battle. Now I knew why. So many of Lisa's updates and the scriptures she posted came to mind and helped to sustain us as we began our cancer journey. God had placed them there to help us remember His sovereignty and to rely on Him. He showed us through Lisa and Neal how strong the Body of Christ truly is, and we felt the strength of our Risen Lord through that same Body of Christ. He had shown us how to be content in all circumstances by the powerful witness Lisa provided through her faithful updates that always gave God the glory. He showed us through them how to glorify God in ALL things! I felt He had now passed the ball to me and it was our turn to use this cancer journey to share His great love and sovereignty with others. God gave us such a marvelous example of what we were to do and how we were to handle this journey long before it began!

God even knew long before we were married that Billy would need an "OCD Trapper Keeper" wife to take notes and keep up with all the details through the multiple consultations with the surgical oncologist, chemo oncologist and radiation oncologist. (Yeah, I had no idea there were so many.) God knew my notes would come in handy to help keep us educated and our family and friends updated. God even timed all of this in such a way that we had our first trip to the Gulf Shores scheduled the week after all of Billy's test and prior to his chemo/radiation treatments began. He knew we would need a reprieve before the battle began.

All my life I have heard God knows what is best; He sees all and knows all; just be patient and wait on Him. As I grew in my Christian walk, I was beginning to gain an understanding that God goes before us. However, it was during our cancer journey that I became absolutely and completely amazed at all the ways God goes before us. I'm sure there are situations I have not seen. God only reveals what my little mind can comprehend at the time and what He did show me, blew me away. Now when I am going into something blind or am not sure what is going on, I walk with much more faith knowing God has gone before me and has me covered!

¹¹ For I know the plans I have for you," declares the LORD, "plans to prosper you and not to harm you, plans to give you hope and a future. ¹² Then you will call upon me and come and pray to me, and I will listen to you. ¹³ You will seek me and find me when you seek me with all your heart.

Jeremiah 29:11-13 (AMP)

When have you heard a small voice telling you to do something you didn't understand only to discover it paid off later?

_____

_____

_____

_____

_____

How has your "hindsight" revealed ways God has gone before you?

_____

_____

_____

_____

_____

_____

How can you walk with more faith knowing God has truly gone before you in all circumstances?

_____

_____

_____

_____

_____

_____

The Birds and the Bees

My husband and I absolutely love to sit on our back porch and watch God's wonderful creations. We have been blessed with a beautiful flower garden where we placed numerous bird feeders. My husband built several bird houses which my niece painted and we have mounted all around our yard and home. In addition to the birds, we have squirrels and chipmunks that frequent our back yard along with a water fountain where we placed a variety of koi and goldfish.

We can sit for hours just watching God's creations. Billy says: "A man can lose a crop like this!" However, after a long week of work, we cannot think of a better way to spend our Saturday mornings than with a hot cup of coffee on our back porch. The Saturday morning after being told Billy had a malignant tumor in his colon we retreated to our favorite place, the back porch. We sat in shock over the news and prayed for God to help us understand. We just sat in silence hoping and praying God would speak to us.

Well, God did speak and He used our favorite activity, nature watching, as the chosen venue. While we have seen many different birds feed in our garden and have even been privileged to see an Indigo Bunting every now and then, we had never seen three Indigo Buntings on the same feeder at the same time. However, on this day God sent us three "blue birds" to remind us of His constant presence IN relationship with us through the trinity. We knew this was not a coincidence but a "God-cidence" as He so carefully placed the three birds (which to this day, we have not seen since) on the shepherd's crook that held this particular feeder. One, two, three in a row, right there, on this day when we so desperately needed to know what this cancer journey held for us.

Later that weekend a large bee flew right in Billy's face and just hovered there looking at him. I became alarmed but Billy just sat there smiling. After the bee flew off, Billy explained to me that it was called a "good news bee." He explained that his mother always told him that if this certain bee came up to your face and "buzzed" you it meant good news was coming your way. I had never heard this but shared it with many others who echoed the same story about the bee. First the trinity of blue birds and now a good news bee! God was using His wonderful creation to speak to us and we now began to feel His peace filling us with hope.

That Monday as we sat in the examining room waiting on Dr. Portera, Jr. to find out just how bad the cancer was, we could feel God's presence and peace. We began to look around the room and noticed that over the chairs we were sitting in were two pictures of blue birds. Then the cancer center where we would spend many hours for Billy to get his chemo and radiation combo treatments had a bird cage right inside the entrance doors. It was full of blue, red, yellow and multi-colored finches and reminded us on each visit of God's presence.

Throughout this journey God used His creatures to remind us of His sovereignty. A year later we spent a week at a beautiful mountain retreat named "Redbird Retreat." Once again God revealed Himself through His creation in the mountains and His creatures. One day that week, Billy and I were discussing his upcoming colonoscopy and he said the only concern he had was they would find something they missed last time. Later that day Billy was "buzzed" by a good news bee . . . this is the only other time we had seen one since that hot July day a year earlier.

After returning home from Redbird Retreat, Billy had his follow-up colonoscopy and we were very excited to hear that NOTHING was found—not even a glimmer of a polyp! PRAISE GOD! He has truly healed Billy and we thank Him for changing us through this journey. We definitely see life differently and believe God used His creation to tell us not to worry. He loves us more than we can imagine and will go to any and all lengths to get us to hear Him. He loves us enough to speak through the birds and bees.

[25] "Therefore I tell you, do not worry about your life, what you will eat or drink; or about your body, what you will wear. Is not life more important than food, and the body more important than clothes? [26]Look at the birds of the air; they do not sow or reap or store away in barns, and

yet your heavenly Father feeds them. Are you not much more valuable than they?

Matthew 6:25-27 (AMP)

When was the last time you slowed down and allowed God to speak to you through His creation?

_____

_____

_____

_____

_____

How has God spoken to you in the ordinary, routine times in your life?

_____

_____

_____

_____

_____

How can you make more time to be in His presence and listen to His voice through His creation?

_____

_____

_____

_____

_____

Angels and Chemo

Whenever you take a new journey you can't help but learn new terms, places, and people. Whether the journey is one that takes you to a new city, state, county, or nation or one that you find yourself on due to circumstances in life, all of them change you in one way or another. Paul found himself on a plethora of journeys. He even found himself on one journey that landed him in prison. Sitting in prison Paul writes to the Philippians and tells them to rejoice in the Lord always and that he has learned to be content in all situations.

Philippians 4:13 happens to be one of my husband's favorite verses and I just love the way it reads in the Amplified Bible: **13 I have strength for all things in Christ Who empowers me [I am ready for anything and equal to anything through Him Who [g] infuses inner strength into me; I am [h] self-sufficient in Christ's sufficiency].** I have to say that my husband is a lot like Paul and he truly does find a way to be content in all situations through Christ. Even when Billy was on his cancer journey he remained positive and upbeat.

One particular time exudes how Billy truly allowed Christ to infuse his inner strength so he could rejoice in all things. We were at the cancer center and Billy was getting his chemo pump which would be housed in a fanny pack and would deliver a constant flow of his weekly chemo. This pump was connected to a port surgically implanted in Billy's chest and would be with him 24/7 for the next six to eight weeks. The nurse told us that most people name their new "buddy" and one lady named hers the albatross and others had named it things I could not repeat. She wanted to know what Billy would name his if at all. Since neither of those styles are Billy, he told her he wanted to keep it positive and would think about it.

Later that day he told me he was going to call it his "angel" since it was providing sustenance that would save his life. So I went to my Bible in search of a verse for him about angels. I wanted to make him an index card with the verse to keep in his fanny pack with his chemo pump. God lead me to a verse that comes from when Jesus was in the garden of Gethsemane on the day of His crucifixion. Jesus was praying: "42 "Father, if you are willing, take this cup from me; yet not my will, but yours be done." 43 **An angel from heaven appeared to him and strengthened him**." Luke 22:42-43 *(AMP)*

Oh how remarkable our God is. Once again He showed us He had gone before us and just like He did with Jesus, He would strengthen Billy through his new angel. While this pump delivered chemo to Billy's body each day we knew God's angel was strengthening him and God was healing him. Like Paul, we rejoiced in the Lord and God's peace filled us and was unrelenting throughout this cancer journey.

⁴Rejoice in the Lord always [delight, gladden yourselves in Him]; again I say, Rejoice!⁽ᴬ⁾ ⁵Let all men know and perceive and recognize your unselfishness (your considerateness, your forbearing spirit). The Lord is near [He is ⁽ᵃ⁾coming soon]. ⁶Do not fret or have any anxiety about anything, but in every circumstance and in everything, by prayer and petition (⁽ᵇ⁾definite requests), with thanksgiving, continue to make your wants known to God. ⁷And God's peace [shall be yours, that ⁽ᶜ⁾tranquil state of a soul assured of its salvation through Christ, and so fearing nothing from God and being content with its earthly lot of whatever sort that is, that peace] which transcends all understanding shall ⁽ᵈ⁾garrison and mount guard over your hearts and minds in Christ Jesus. ⁸For the rest, brethren, whatever is true, whatever is worthy of reverence and is honorable and seemly, whatever is just, whatever is pure, whatever is lovely and lovable, whatever is kind and winsome and gracious, if there is any virtue and excellence, if there is anything worthy of praise, think on and weigh and take account of these things [fix your minds on them].

Philippians 4: 3-8 (AMP)

What do you need to do to be "self-sufficient in Christ sufficiency"?

_____

_____

_____

_____

_____

_____

What has been or is the most difficult circumstance in your life to find joy?

_____

_____

_____

_____

_____

_____

What do you need to "fix your mind" on in order to find God's peace?

_____

_____

_____

_____

_____

God's Orchestra

I can remember hearing that we now live in a "microwave society." This saying came about due to the how fast you could heat and cook your food using a microwave in place of a conventional oven and how society now expected everything to be as fast as the microwave. I was particularly feeling part of this microwave society as I explained to my friend about the "fast and furious pace of my life." He graciously listened and then reminded me to slow down and take the time to see God's orchestration in my life.

This really played on my heart all that week as I struggled to grasp what God's orchestration looked like. As I drew on the one memory I had of going to the Atlanta Symphony Orchestra, I finally obtained a clear picture. A picture that not only could I see, I could hear and feel it. Here it is, God's Orchestration. I would tell you to close your eyes and picture this . . . . but, yeah, hard to read with your eyes closed. So take your time and allow God to form the picture and sounds in your mind and heart.

Your life—the orchestra hall—The orchestra is warming up . . . all instruments playing notes and chords. A cacophony of sounds as everyone is hustling around to get in place, get in tune, all trying to be ready and in place on time.

The maestro steps into place, lifts his hands and ALL get quiet. Not a sound. All eyes are on the maestro. All wait expectantly for his direction. Then without a sound, he begins to motion for each instrument to join him in producing the most beautiful music. He leads and everyone follows. The individual sounds of all instruments coming together in beautiful harmony. All continue to watch his every move as he conducts in perfect timing producing music that touches the soul!

Our God—our Jesus—our Maestro steps into our lives lifting His nail pierced hands and is waiting for us to get quiet—waiting for our eyes to be fixed on Him—waiting for our hearts to expectantly await His direction so He can conduct our lives to produce His beautiful music that will touch souls.

May we all "be still and know He is God." May we all join together and allow Him to conduct our lives in His perfect timing. As we begin each new week, I pray protection over you all as satan will try to steal this vision in the busyness of each day. I challenge myself and all of you to take time out of each day to actually "eat lunch" and not work through it; take time to see His people that He has placed in your path; take time to see His outstretched, nail pierced hands just waiting and longing to conduct your life. I know it isn't going to be easy but I also know the end result is worth it!

³⁸Now while they were on their way, it occurred that Jesus entered a certain village, and a woman named Martha received and welcomed Him into her house. ³⁹And she had a sister named Mary, who seated herself at the Lord's feet and was listening to His teaching. ⁴⁰But Martha [overly occupied and too busy] was distracted with much serving; and she came up to Him and said, Lord, is it nothing to You that my sister has left me to serve alone? Tell her then to help me [to lend a hand and do her part along with me]! ⁴¹But the Lord replied to her by saying, Martha, Martha, you are anxious and troubled about many things; ⁴²There is need of only one or but [a]a few things. Mary has chosen the good portion [b]that which is to her advantage], which shall not be taken away from her.

Luke 10:38-42 (AMP)

What makes up the "cacophony of sounds" in your life?

_____

_____

_____

_____

_____

What directions do you need to wait "expectantly" on from God?

_____

_____

_____

_____

_____

_____

What do you need to do in order to have your eyes fixed on the Maestro so you will be in perfect timing with Him?

_____

_____

_____

_____

_____

_____

Healing in the Journey

One of the saddest parts of our cancer journey was sitting in the cancer center and watching the endless number of people who would come through the door for treatment each day. Once you have been there and experienced the fear, anger, hurt, anxiety, and shock of a cancer diagnosis, you view cancer patients and caregivers in a whole new light. For the first time in our life, we could identify with them. Their expressions and mannerisms were a dead giveaway as to where they were in their journey. Just like ours the first time we entered the center, the look of helplessness coupled with hope precedes you through the doors.

You feel like you are watching a show on TV as you move through the waiting room wondering how you ended up there. One of the first places we went after Billy's diagnosis was to our church. We met our pastor and some friends there and our pastor prayed over Billy. He prayed for Jesus to miraculously heal Billy. Yet here we were in a cancer center with all of these people, some of who were Christians and some who weren't. We truly believe in miracles as we had prayed and been part of some that God had performed in our friends lives. So why were we here? Why did Billy have to go through this? Was our faith not strong enough? Were we not good enough to get a miracle of instant healing?

Then one day during my quiet time, God lead me to Luke 17 where Jesus met the ten lepers who asked Jesus to heal them. Unlike many of the healing miracles Jesus had performed, He did not reach out and touch them nor did He instantly heal them. Instead He told them to go to the priest. They were not healed until they were on their way to the priest. Back in those days the priest was the only person who could proclaim a leper was healed. Imagine how depressing it must have been for the priest to mostly see the disease and not the healing. Now imagine the priest once the ten arrived and he was able to make that healing proclamation.

God used this to show us that not all of Jesus' healings were "immediate"—here Jesus sent them to the priest and "as they went" they were healed. God showed me that there are times that it glorifies Him more for us to "walk the path as healed people" and to praise "God in a loud voice" than it is to be healed immediately. He also revealed that there are times that He uses us to encourage those who are in charge of the ceremonies of healing, priest then but doctors these days. They too need to see God is working in and through them as they use the gifts God gave them.

Now as we would enter the cancer center we knew God had placed us there to walk as healed people and to sing His praises so others could be encouraged. We were so blessed that all of Billy's oncologist were Christians and we knew God was using us to strengthen their confidence that God was working through them to heal His people. We knew we were to hold fast to God's words and confidently know that "as Billy goes" God was healing him and was using this journey to bring God glory. Our job was to sing His praises LOUDLY and walk as healed people along the way. PRAISE GOD FOR HIS WORD! What strength and encouragement God provided us through it.

11 Now on his way to Jerusalem, Jesus traveled along the border between Samaria and Galilee. 12 As he was going into a village, ten men who had leprosy[a] met him. They stood at a distance 13 and called out in a loud voice, "Jesus, Master, have pity on us!" 14 When he saw them, he said, "Go, show yourselves to the priests." And as they went, they were cleansed. 15 One of them, when he saw he was healed, came back, praising God in a loud voice. 16 He threw himself at Jesus' feet and thanked him—and he was a Samaritan. 17 Jesus asked, "Were not all ten cleansed? Where are the other nine? 18 Was no one found to return and give praise to God except this foreigner?" 19 Then he said to him, "Rise and go; your faith has made you well."

Luke 17: 11-19 (AMP)

What in your life causes you to feel unworthy of God's healing?

_____

_____

_____

_____

_____

_____

What do you need to do to walk as a healed person?

_____

_____

_____

_____

_____

_____

How can God use your praises to encourage others along your journey?

_____

_____

_____

_____

_____

_____

Seeing the Wheat

Three years ago Carla, my very best friend and prayer partner, gave me a Christmas gift I just opened today. Three years ago my husband became the principal at the school where we were both teaching and I was in the process of adding my EdS in Leadership so I could move out of the classroom. Now you have to understand that our high school is the only high school in our county! While there was not a nepotism policy that would prevent me from keeping my job, his promotion to principal meant my career plans came to a halt unless I left and went to another county.

I live in Dade County, Georgia, which is in the farthest northwest corner of the state. Alabama and Tennessee provide two of our borders and the closest county in Georgia would be a thirty to forty minute drive up and over a mountain! While I was thrilled for Billy, I struggled with what this meant for my career. Other than God, only Carla knew all the ugly truth of my struggles. She was that person God gave me that I could let it all out and she could be totally honest and set me straight after I got it out. So for Christmas she gave me this gift that I was to keep and allow God to use to help me to view my future like a child waiting to open a present. She placed a note on the outside of the box that said:

"This box represents the gift that is yours as you travel down this path of your career. Only God knows what He has in store for you—but whatever it is, we can be sure that He will give you a desire for it as He reveals it to you. The box itself is a children's shoe box—symbolic of the fact that we are to follow his instruction with the simple faith that a child might have. I look forward to the day He lets you open your box my dear . . . but in the meantime, know that you have my love, prayers, tears, frustrations and support as you follow His path—don't forget to let God lead . . . He's a much better dancer than you, I am sure! ☺"

As I was struggling to write this devotion and getting ready to quit, God lead me to open my gift. Inside was a beautiful note from Carla that said:

"My dearest Susan,

If you are reading this, then you have no doubt been allowed to open the gift box God gave you this year (2007). What a mystery it has been—how have all of the events of the past few years played into God's plan for you? I have no doubt that whatever God has given you, it is His very best because that's what He wants for me and you. Merry Christmas to you, no matter what time of the year it is—I'm so blessed to travel this journey with you.

All My Love, Carla

Billy retired and I finally got a position in leadership and thought this was the time to open the gift. But, Carla's question in her note kept ringing in my head. "How have all of the events of the past few years played into God's plan for you?" Oh, I get it! It wasn't about the job, it was about the journey; it was about seeing the wheat! Now I knew what God wanted me to write.

You see, after Billy was named principal in January, he was diagnosed with cancer in July of the same year. While I was trying to support my husband and help him in every way possible, some people saw it as me trying to run the school. Now not only were we dealing with cancer, we were dealing with the spiritual warfare going on at work. So, how have all of the events of the past few years played into God's plan for me? God allowed satan to sift me like wheat!

Since the Bible was written before modern machinery, I decided to research how wheat was sifted in the old days. First the wheat was laid out and threshed. That means it was beaten until the grain was separated from the husk. Then it was tossed in the air so the chaff, which is much lighter than the grain, would blow away in the wind. Then all that is left is the wheat.

At first glance, this process makes you want to say: "Yep that sounds about right. Having your career come to a screeching halt and your husband diagnosed with cancer would make anyone feel like they had been laid out, beaten and tossed about!" However, seeing the wheat must become your lens throughout the entire process.

First, satan must have permission and Christ gave permission because He knows the wheat is all that will be left at the end of the process. Satan thinks it will be the chaff but Christ KNOWS it will be the wheat! So God taught me to focus on seeing the wheat and glorifying God with shouts of praise as satan attacked us through this cancer and the spiritual warfare at work. There's nothing sweeter than singing victory songs during the heat of battle.

What's more, you know what wheat is used to make? That's right, bread! How wonderful it is that the Bread of Life, Jesus, sees us as wheat. Like Him, we are made to rise and like any good baker, He never forgets we are in the oven nor does He leave us in there too long. He knows the exact moment and time that we will be perfectly baked and ready to serve. Remember, Christ told Simon that he was praying for him and He knew his faith would not fail!

Subsequently, satan hopes that we will only see the chaff. However, Christ gently blows it away as satan tries to shake our faith. Many times I knew I was beating myself up by focusing on the people and circumstances and not on God. Even so, Christ never sends us to battle alone and He sends us to battle totally equipped with HIS armor. So many times when all I could see was the chaff, I would get an e-mail, phone call, note or visit from one of Christ's warriors telling me that I had just been on their heart and they had been praying for me. I learned to put on the armor of God every day and to wait for reinforcements; they were on their way!

While I would never wish sifting on anyone, I would never trade these past years of sifting for anything. It was through this sifting that I discovered there was more to life than working; cancer will do that to you. It was through sifting that I was able to see the wheat and write all the e-mails sharing how God was sustaining us through it all. It was through the e-mails that I was encouraged to write and it was through putting on God's armor that I dug into His word and I could hear His call to write.

So to Carla and all of the reinforcements: Thank you for going to battle with us—your prayers helped us hold up the shield of faith and provided us with His word as we lifted His sword. Your prayers covered us like the breast plate of righteousness and the helmet of salvation and protected our hearts from what was said and what we say; your prayers held firm the belt of truth so we could focus on it and the shoes of peace so we could walk in the peace of Christ and His promise that HE himself is praying for us and that the battle is already won! Thank you for helping me to see the wheat.

31 "Simon, Simon, Satan has asked to sift you[a] as wheat. 32 But I have prayed for you, Simon, that your faith may not fail. And when you have turned back, strengthen your brothers."

Luke 22: 31-32 (AMP)

5 Trust in the Lord with all your heart and lean not on your own understanding.

Proverbs 3:5 (AMP)

When was a time in your life you were sifted?

_____

_____

_____

_____

_____

_____

What chaff did you see blown away due to the sifting?

_____

_____

_____

_____

_____

_____

What is God trying to show you through the wheat in your life?

_____

_____

_____

_____

_____

_____

Scarcely Abundant?

It was summer and time for our seasonal Courage to Teach Retreat. What would this season bring? Where would God take me on this retreat? I packed my bags and drove to Amacalola Falls, Georgia with great anticipation. All along the way the scenery was bursting with lush green trees and grass, while the fullness of the flowers added wonderful splashes of color. What a beautiful sight to see the scarcity of winter was now lost in the abundance of the rich, bright colors of summer.

As we sought to grasp the huge dichotomy between abundance and scarcity, God took me down memory lane to my BCR (before Christ ruled) days. Clearly the memories of shopping ran through my mind and how it seemed I never had enough money. There was always something else I felt I just needed to have and the lack of money didn't slow me down. I had plenty of plastic and it was accepted just as readily as cash, so, why not? The terms "restraint" and "budget" never seemed to overtake my wants.

This pattern continued until I ran up my debt up to over $10,000.00 and I was living "hand to mouth." Almost every dime I made was spent before I got my paycheck. The more I tried to fill the emptiness of my life with "things" I bought, the bigger the hole seemed to get. I didn't have enough money to fill that hole and now I barely had enough money to buy food after I paid my bills. I certainly could say that my money was scarce compared to the abundant bills.

Gaining control of my spending had to become a priority, so, I consolidated my bills, got rid of my credit cards, and asked my mother to help me set up a budget. She taught me how to set aside money for all of my bills and then to get the remaining amount in cash. I had five envelopes that I kept in my dresser drawer. Since payday came the last day of each month, after paying my bills I would divide the remaining cash by the number of weeks in that month and place that amount into each envelope.

Every Monday I would take the cash from one envelope in the drawer and that was all I could spend that week. This is when I learned to drink water instead of soft drinks or tea; water was free. I learned to not go to the mall or any other stores where I would find temptations like clothes, shoes, decorative items for my apartment, etc. If there was something I wanted, I learned to put some cash aside from each week and at the end of the month, if it was still there, to treat myself and purchase the item.

While the huge hole was still in my life, it was no longer running my life and I was learning obedience and control. About this time is when I allowed Christ out of the guest room to rule my life. It was absolutely amazing how the small amount of cash for each week seemed to last longer and go further. No, I didn't get a raise or take on a second job. That huge hole was now being filled with Christ and I no longer had the desire to run out and go shopping. I no longer felt I had to get something "just in case" I needed it. The temptations to fill that hole with things of this world waned as my relationship with Christ grew stronger.

The debt began to shrink and Christ introduced me to stewardship. Now I longed not only to be out of debt, but to be a good steward of Christ's money. I even began to regularly give to the church and wondered if I would ever be able to truly tithe, give 10% of my earnings back to Christ. What was amazing was that the more I gave, the less I needed but it seemed the more I would get. So now the scarcity of my money was abundantly flowing through Christ and He was filling that hole to overflowing. So my financial state was "scarcely abundant."

This oxymoron description for my financial state carried over into my emotional and spiritual life. The more I gave of myself to God, the more He blessed me. I learned that the scarcity comes when I place my vision, thoughts, and values on things of this world and lose sight of God's promise to always be there and to provide just enough light for the step I'm on. Whenever I would try to see more than His light reveals, the fear of not having or being enough would come creeping back.

I learned that by keeping my eyes where God shines His light revealed the abundance of His grace, mercy and love. It was only through His light that I could see the abundance He had given me in my family, friends, home and job. By focusing on His promises, gifts and light it gave me the faith to not look into the dark dim edges around the light but to walk only on the step He illuminates and having the faith that He will continue to provide. I now could discern between my wants and needs.

God has truly given back to me what the locus has eaten. He said it, promised it and He continues to provide. As long as I stay focused on the step He illumines and no more or no less, He reveals His gifts, joyously proclaiming His goodness and abounding love. The more I give to God, the less I need of this world. I now know that God is enough! True to His word the treasures I store in Him will always return to me abundantly. He is all I need!

¹³Someone from the crowd said to Him, Master, order my brother to divide the inheritance and share it with me. ¹⁴But He told him, Man, who has appointed Me a judge or umpire and divider over you? ¹⁵And He said to them, Guard yourselves and keep free from all covetousness (the immoderate desire for wealth, the greedy longing to have more); for a man's life does not consist in and is not derived from possessing ⁽ᵃ⁾overflowing abundance or that which is ⁽ᵇ⁾over and above his needs. ¹⁶Then He told them a parable, saying, The land of a rich man was fertile and yielded plentifully. ¹⁷And he considered and debated within himself, What shall I do? I have no place [in which] to gather together my harvest. ¹⁸And he said, I will do this: I will pull down my storehouses and build larger ones, and there I will store all [c]my grain or produce and my goods.

19And I will say to my soul, Soul, you have many good things laid up, enough] for many years. Take your ease; eat, drink, and enjoy yourself merrily. 20But God said to him, You fool! This very night [d] they [the messengers of God] will demand your soul of you; and all the things that you have prepared, whose will they be?(A)21So it is with the one who continues to lay up and hoard possessions for himself and is not rich [in his relation] to God [this is how he fares].

Luke 12:13-21 (AMP)

19 "Do not store up for yourselves treasures on earth, where moth and rust destroy, and where thieves break in and steal. 20But store up for yourselves treasures in heaven, where moth and rust do not destroy, and where thieves do not break in and steal. 21For where your treasure is, there your heart will be also.

Matthew 6: 19-21 (AMP)

How are you trying to fill the emptiness in your life?

_____

_____

_____

_____

_____

_____

What do you consider the treasures of your life?

_____

_____

_____

_____

_____

_____

How can you become a better steward of your financial and spiritual life?

_____

_____

_____

_____

_____

_____

Strolling

After reading Mary Oliver's poem "The Summer Day" during one of our Courage to Teach retreats, we were presented with several questions, but two stood out to me. When do you stroll through life, and when have you been idle and blessed? This retreat came the first year Billy and I were married and I was working in Dalton, Georgia. My commute was two hours each day, an hour there and an hour home, if traffic allowed. I would rise early and be on the road by 6:00 am and would not return home until 6:30/7:00 pm. My life consisted of driving, work, driving, workout, occasionally getting my nails done, dinner and bed. Here I sat at a retreat faced with words like "stroll" and "idle"

Boy was God stepping all over my toes and entire foot. Who had time to stroll and be idle? Since Trenton had only one high school with only one Technology Education program and it was filled, I did feel blessed to have a job that was closer than driving to Kennesaw (where I lived before Billy and I married). But come on, stroll and idle? Unmistakably God was using this retreat to tell me to slow down and not pack my day so full. He was showing me I had become mechanical in my being as I ran to accomplish each task.

Okay, to stroll means to take each moment slowly and calmly enough so that I am relaxed enough to actually see, hear, and feel the wonderful blessings God had placed so deliberately in my path. I needed to take time to not only hear the birds, but to take time to stop and find the bird who sings such beautiful songs and take time to watch how they sing and fly. I was to slow down and take time to not just see and hear the anger of those in pain but to see the fear and pain behind the angry voice. Then I was to take the time to help or just pray for their release from the pain and/or fear.

I looked up the definition of "idle" on Google and it says "not in action or in work." So, I was not only to slow down but to stop? God showed me how satan uses the busyness of life to cause confusion and noise. The more confusion and noise in my life, the less focused I could be on God and the less I could see His blessings. I knew I had to stop the noise and take time to wonder in silence. Take time to clear my head so I could see God's blessings. I decided to use my drive time to reflect and be silent, to stop the noise. Yes, that meant no radio or cell phone on my commuter!

Doing this helped me to begin and end my day with being idle and blessed. I would only plan one extra item on my daily agenda and made sure I had time for my family. Driving in silence helped me to decompress before I got home. I was able to be the wife and stepmom God called me to be instead of the frazzled, worn out employee they had been getting. I began filling my weekends with family time and learned to stroll through them savoring each moment. Then, on my morning drives in silence, I could continue that stroll as I went into my work week.

To stroll and be idle and blessed means that I take one day at a time, no, one moment at a time. It means to stop the noise and look, listen and feel God's presence, His presence in nature, people, and in self. My friend Carla reminds me that we are human "beings" not human "doers." So, stop, look, listen and feel . . . stroll and be idle and blessed, my friend.

²² Because of the LORD's great love we are not consumed, for his compassions never fail. ²³ They are new every morning; great is your faithfulness. ²⁴ I say to myself, "The LORD is my portion; therefore I will wait for him." ²⁵ The LORD is good to those whose hope is in him, to the one who seeks him; ²⁶ it is good to wait quietly for the salvation of the LORD. ²⁷ It is good for a man to bear the yoke while he is young. ²⁸ Let him sit alone in silence, for the LORD has laid it on him.

Lamentations 3: 22-28 (AMP)

When do you stroll through life, and when have you been idle and blessed?

_____

_____

_____

_____

_____

_____

What do you need to do to stop the noise and take time to wonder?

_____

_____

_____

_____

_____

_____

Take this time to plan your weekend to include time to stroll and be idle . . . . what will you do and what will you NOT do?

_____

_____

_____

_____

_____

_____

Cracked Pots

Early in my Christian walk I fell in love with Amy Grant and the song "All I Ever Have to Be." To this day God uses this song to speak to me and remind me that I am His daughter of grace. In her song, Amy Grant reminds me that "all I have to be is what You made me. Any more or less would be a step out of your plan. As you daily recreate me, help me always keep in mind that all I have to be is what you made me." She helps me to remember that I am what I am today because of God's unmerited pardon for all of my mistakes, sins.

I am what I am today because God used my sins to shape me into a vessel He would fill and use to show others His marvelous light. My wholeness encompasses my victories and my defeats, my treasures and my mess, my beauty and my imperfections. Yet God only sees my treasure as my mistakes and sins are washed away with Jesus blood. He only sees what He created me to be. So are my mistakes imperfections or are they the lack of me being what He created me to be?

Are my mistakes me trying to be something I am not? If I can truly be what He created me to be then I am whole. Yet I must accept my past, warts and all, and I must also forgive myself as Christ has forgiven me. When I look back I should see a precious Child of God, His daughter. I should see me as God sees me and not fear my past. I must learn from the mistakes and rejoice in His grace and mercy for yet another day to allow Him to "daily recreate" me.

My wholeness is where the treasure resides because the treasure is Christ's forgiveness, love, grace and mercy that have made me what I am today. It is because of my mistakes and His mercy and grace that I am able to share the same love, mercy and grace with others. It is through my story that I can witness for Christ and lead others to Him. My wholeness is only because Christ put my broken pieces back together. He did so in such a way that it is not perfect. He left cracks so His light could shine through me. It is His light that draws others and allows me to be His witness. It is the cracks that allows His light to shine through me and enables me to extend to others His love and forgiveness.

My treasure is an old broken pot that has been pieced back together with Christ love, grace and mercy. Some pieces are missing because He no longer remembers my sin. Those holes leave room for Him to shine through me so others may see Him and not this old broken pot. Yes, my treasure resides in my wholeness, imperfections and all. It is only when Christ fills this old pot with His light and becomes more than I that the pot is seen as whole. It is then that I can sing: "And I realize the good in me, is only there because of who You are." Thank you, Amy Grant, for allowing God to work through you and provide us a song that is such a beautiful reminder that all we have to be is what God created us to be!

Susan A. Millican

¹O LORD, you have searched me [thoroughly] and have known me. ²You know my down sitting and my uprising; You understand my thought afar off.⁽ᴬ⁾ ³You sift and search out my path and my lying down, and You are acquainted with all my ways. ⁴For there is not a word in my tongue [still unuttered], but, behold, O Lord, You know it altogether.⁽ᴮ ⁵You have beset me and shut me in—behind and before, and You have laid Your hand upon me. ⁶Your [infinite] knowledge is too wonderful for me; it is high above me, I cannot reach it. ⁷Where could I go from Your Spirit? Or where could I flee from Your presence? ⁸If I ascend up into heaven, You are there; if I make my bed in Sheol (the place of the dead), behold, You are there.⁽ᶜ⁾ ⁹If I take the wings of the morning or dwell in the uttermost parts of the sea, ¹⁰Even there shall Your hand lead me, and Your right hand shall hold me. ¹¹If I say, Surely the darkness shall cover me and the night shall be [the only] light about me, ¹²Even the darkness hides nothing from You, but the night shines as the day; the darkness and the light are both alike to You.⁽ᴰ⁾ ¹³For You did form my inward parts; You did knit me together in my mother's womb.¹⁴I will confess and praise You for You are fearful and wonderful and for the awful wonder of my birth! Wonderful are Your works, and that my inner self knows right well. ¹⁵My frame was not hidden from You when I was being formed in secret [and] intricately and curiously wrought [as if embroidered with various colors] in the depths of the earth [a region of darkness and mystery]. ¹⁶Your eyes saw my unformed substance, and in Your book all the days [of my life] were written before ever they took shape, when as yet there was

none of them. [17] How precious and weighty also are Your thoughts to me, O God! How vast is the sum of them!
Psalm 139: 1-17 (AMP)

What is it you need to forgive yourself for and allow God to shine through?

_____

_____

_____

_____

_____

_____

What broken pieces do you need to allow Christ to put back together?

_____

_____

_____

_____

_____

_____

What do you need to do to allow Christ to become more than you so His light will shine through your cracks?

_____

_____

_____

_____

_____

Give 'Em More

One day as I was prayer walking around my church I could see all of these families entering our church. There was a carnival being held that night which we hoped would bring in new families. I started to pray for this event and the workers and families attending. Since I had not been inside and did not know many of the families, I struggled on specifically what to pray. So, I walked in silence waiting and listening. That is when the Holy Spirit spoke to me and gave me a song to sing as I walked.

The song was not based on anything specific to pray; it was about asking God to "Give 'em more." I could hear it over and over:

Give 'em MORE than what they came for let them see Your face;
Give 'em MORE.
Give 'em MORE than what they came for show Your glory and Your grace;
Give 'em MORE.

The more I walked and listened, the more lines I was given:

Surround them with Your presence, and fill them with Your
joy.
Give 'em MORE.
Let Your Holy Spirit move and soften up their hearts.
Renew their broken spirits and heal their wounded souls.
Give 'em MORE!
Open up their hearts that they may receive all of Your
blessings and Your peace.
Give 'em more.
Give 'em MORE than what they came for.

What an incredible experience this turned out to be. It
brought to light that when I don't know what to pray to ask
the Holy Spirit and He will pray for me. It made me realize
how in trying to be specific in my prayers I was putting God
in a box. It made me wonder how often I boxed Jesus in with
my human limitations. Our God is so awesome and He is
limitless. He knows no bounds; nonetheless, we humans put
so many constraints and limits on Him. We ask for what we
think is best. We ask for what we want. We ask for what we
know is within our bounds. We limit God because we only
ask for what we know, can see and can do.

Oh, how silly we must appear to Jesus when He has something
so much better for us and we have our hearts and minds set on
what we think. How silly it must look to a financial advisor
when you buy a Pinto when you could afford a Cadillac all
because the Pinto is all you know! How silly we are that we
put stock in advice from others but we fail to allow God free
reign because He might lead us where we have never been.

Oh to let God out of the box and fully trust Him to supply all our needs. How wonderful would that be? God's gift that day was a song I would sing in my head and heart for years to come; one I would sing over our church, my classroom and school, and over friends and family. I pray that as you have read each page of this book that God has given you more than you expected. I pray that He will continue to give you more as you take the lid off the box and release Him to fully reign in your life. May you experience the full blessings of our Lord and Savior and may you shout them out with joy as you walk with Him each day. Blessings and love to you!

96I have seen that everything [human] has its limits and end [no matter how extensive, noble, and excellent]; but Your commandment is exceedingly broad and extends without limits [into eternity].

Psalm 119: 96 (AMP)

What does the box you put God in look like?

_____

_____

_____

_____

_____

_____

Where in your life do you need to give God "free reign?"

_____

_____

_____

_____

_____

_____

Take this time to just allow the Holy Spirit to pray for you . . . .
record what you hear God telling you:

_____

_____

_____

_____

_____

_____